Using SOLO
as a Framework for Teaching

A case study in maximising achievement in science

Steve Martin

essential
resources

| Title: | Using SOLO as a Framework for Teaching |
| | A case study in maximising achievement in science |

Author: Steve Martin

Editor: Tanya Tremewan

Designer: Diane Whitford

Book code: 5618

ISBN: 978-1-927143-55-1

Published: 2011

Publisher: Essential Resources Educational Publishers Limited

United Kingdom:	**Australia:**	**New Zealand:**
Units 8–10 Parkside	PO Box 906	PO Box 5036
Shortgate Lane	Strawberry Hills	Invercargill
Laughton BN8 6DG	NSW 2012	
ph: 0845 3636 147	ph: 1800 005 068	ph: 0800 087 376
fax: 0845 3636 148	fax: 1800 981 213	fax: 0800 937 825

Websites: www.essentialresourcesuk.com
www.essentialresources.com.au
www.essentialresources.co.nz

About the author: Steve Martin received the Prime Minister's Award for Excellence in Science Teaching, New Zealand's top teaching award, in November 2010 in recognition of the work he has done inspiring students to higher levels of achievement through the innovative use of SOLO Taxonomy and ICT. He won the Most Inspiring Individual Award in the 2011 New Zealand Innovators Awards for his virtual lesson project and the Microsoft Distinguished Teacher Award in 2009. Steve is an Honorary Professional Teaching Fellow at Auckland University and has been teaching for 17 years. He holds a BSc(Hons) and a Master's degree in Educational Leadership and Management.

Foreword

It is so much easier to sit in my academic office, pore over research evidence, build models and test theories. It is so much harder to take the outcomes of these endeavours and put them into practice – and then to evaluate the impact of these ideas on student learning. The big ideas in my work include ensuring there is cognitive complexity, learning intentions, success criteria, student assessment capabilities, progression, feedback and self-regulated learning. Steve Martin has found a way to use these powerful notions in the classroom and this book is an account of his methods, thinking and success.

I have been so impressed with his way of conceiving how to make a difference, how to then engage students in the complexities of high school science, and how the students of all abilities and dispositions (naughty to gifted) become turned on to Steve's passion. He has presented an excellent system to take the major ideas and use them not only to plan, but also to plan with the students. His success rate in the national assessment system is renown – not just by enhancing the engaged and effective students who come into his classroom, but also by engaging the dispossessed, the disgruntled and the disinterested students. This is the true success of a teacher – and now you can see how he thinks, how he sees the task of teaching and learning, and see his mind frame about making a difference to student learning.

John Biggs and Kevin Collis developed the SOLO Taxonomy in the 1970s. They started in poetry, and then moved to all areas of the curriculum. The SOLO method has been used at the university level, in developing rubrics for writing and for evaluating teacher effectiveness, in gifted programmes and in special education classes. We have used it extensively in developing our national assessment reporting system. It is the case, however, that SOLO is not generally well known. Steve has brought SOLO alive, shows its power and simplicity, and has written persuasively that others should think, do and enjoy as he has. A model of theory into practice, and how practice has informed theory; a model of research informed teaching; and an excellent system for knowing thy impact!

Professor John Hattie
Director, Melbourne Education Research Institute (MERI) and Associate Dean (Research)

Acknowledgements

The greatest acknowledgement must go to my family: Cherie, my wife, who has made many sacrifices to allow me to pursue my SOLO journey and has provided me with tremendous support and encouragement; and William, our son, who inspires me to help all students enjoy success and prepare them for a life of learning.

I thank Pam Hook and Julie Mills for their work 'Hooked on Thinking' which introduced me to the potential of the SOLO taxonomy and on which the Learning Log and the identification of learning intentions and success criteria under the levels of SOLO is based. I strongly advise all to visit their website www.hooked-on-thinking.com. I would also like to thank the staff at Auckland University who have been incredibly supportive and encouraging: Maree Davies, Frank Walton, Tony Hunt and Graeme Aitken.

I would like to especially thank my colleagues at Howick College who have been instrumental in creating a very supportive environment. Special thanks to Ian Parker for his endless passion and enthusiasm, he has been an inspirational mentor during my time at the school. I value and appreciate the learning conversations and guidance of Janice Wright.

There have been staff members at other schools who have placed considerable effort and thought into using the ideas outlined in this book and I would like to thank Barbara Warne and Mark Thornton-Pett for their comments and feedback.

Finally, I am indebted to the inspiration, guidance and incredible support of John Hattie.

Contents

Introduction

It is every teacher's dream and desire to do their best for their students. Yet rarely do teachers feel they have come to the point where they cannot do any more to improve the learning for their students. Indeed, it is easy to become overwhelmed by the numerous aspects of teaching that will potentially enhance student learning. Many teachers embrace new teaching interventions but too often fail to embed them into their classroom over a sustained period. There are many reasons for such difficulties, including: no or little perceived gain compared with the effort required to maintain the intervention, time constraints within a busy curriculum, the abandonment of the intervention in favour of another, apparently better one, no link to an overall model of learning and a lack of clarity. On reflection over the last 17 years of my own teaching career I can cite these reasons as to why I continued to feel that I was going round in circles and making no real progress in my teaching.

This situation has changed with the use of a framework called SOLO Taxonomy which provides a clear structure that can be applied to all aspects of teaching and learning. It allows the development of challenging hierarchal learning intentions and brings clarity to both the teacher and the student as to what the intended learning is to be.

Using SOLO as a Framework for Teaching shows how this model of learning can be transferred into everyday teaching and learning in a simple but sophisticated way. Teachers are obviously aware of theories of teaching and learning but how well can they articulate how such theories influence their teaching? Ironically, the complex demands of the job make it difficult to spend time thinking deeply about practice and where the different theories fit in. The aim of this book therefore is to help make a powerful model of learning an integral part of teaching and learning in the classroom.

SOLO Taxonomy in action

The Structure of Observed Learning Outcomes (SOLO) Taxonomy was devised by John Biggs and Kevin Collis in the 1970s and 1980s. It is a model of learning that describes levels of thinking that can be observed and that can become increasingly more complex and difficult. Its original application was in the identification of the sophistication of a learner's thinking.

SOLO Taxonomy consists of four key levels:

1. The **unistructural** level describes outcomes that require the learner to identify or describe a single fact or idea.

    For example: Carbon dioxide is found in trace amounts in the atmosphere (0.038%).

2. The **multistructural** level describes outcomes where the learner identifies, lists or describes several relevant facts or ideas but has made no connection between them.

    For example: Carbon dioxide acts as a thermal insulator. It can be found in trace amounts in the atmosphere (0.038%) and is considered to be a greenhouse gas.

3. The **relational** level includes outcomes where the learner has made connections between several relevant facts.

    For example: Carbon dioxide, which is found in trace amounts in the atmosphere, contributes to the greenhouse effect. It allows the sun's rays to pass through it which in turn heat up the earth's surface. Carbon dioxide then acts as a thermal insulator, slowing down the escape of this heat and so causing the greenhouse effect.

4. The **extended abstract** level includes outcomes where the learner has made connections between facts or ideas (relational) and has then linked it to some other concept or theory.

    For example: Carbon dioxide, which is found in trace amounts in the atmosphere, contributes to the greenhouse effect. It allows the sun's rays to pass through it which in turn heat up the earth's surface. Carbon dioxide then acts as a thermal insulator, slowing down the escape of this heat and so causing the greenhouse effect. The theory of global warming states that the increase of greenhouse gases such as carbon dioxide is leading to higher global temperatures and it predicts that this is the reason for unpredictable weather patterns, increased rate of melting in the ice caps and rising sea-levels.

Figure 1 identifies sample verbs that are associated with each level of SOLO Taxonomy. It also recognises the prestructural level at which competence has not yet been achieved; at this level, therefore, verbs that indicate understanding are not applicable.

Figure 1: SOLO Taxonomy with sample verbs indicating levels of understanding

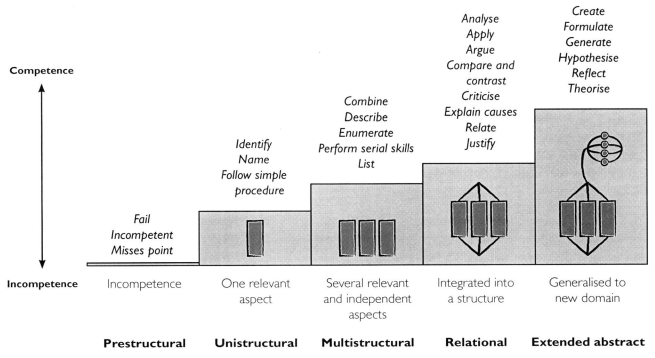

Adapted from: johnbiggs.com.au

We can then use SOLO Taxonomy to formulate questions or tasks. For example, with reference to the previous example of carbon dioxide, Example 1 presents some questions that might be formed using the taxonomy as a framework.

Example 1: Questions about carbon dioxide at the different SOLO levels

	Unistructural	Identify one property of carbon dioxide.
	Multistructural	Describe two or more properties of carbon dioxide.
	Relational	Relate carbon dioxide to the greenhouse effect.
	Extended abstract	What are the possible consequences of the increasing levels of carbon dioxide in the atmosphere?

The sample verbs shown in Figure 1 above are repeatedly used throughout this book to help identify the level of thinking that the teacher is targeting. The method provides a simple, clear and logical framework for a whole range of purposes including: learning intentions, success criteria, differentiation, self assessment, peer assessment, goal setting, measuring progress, motivation, formative assessment and questioning. All of these will be explained in greater detail in this book.

Surface and deep learning

The unistructural and multistructural levels can be considered surface levels of thinking as they involve little cognitive processing. In the questions set out in Example 1 (page 7), the students are simply required to identify or describe properties of carbon dioxide. As the cognitive activity required at the relational and extended abstract levels is markedly higher, these levels are categorised as causing deep learning.

It is important to note that students will use both levels of thinking, surface and deep, in their learning. There is no claim that surface knowledge is not worthwhile; indeed the SOLO model assumes surface knowledge when students relate and extend their understanding. Individual students may prefer a surface or a deep approach but teachers should strive to facilitate both in the classroom. The key is not to develop only one or the other but to achieve the desired proportions of surface and deep learning in any series of lessons.

Achieving those proportions is an important consideration in teaching. Too much time spent at the lower end of SOLO Taxonomy, facilitating surface learning, will demotivate students as activities with this focus soon lose their challenge. Conversely, if too little time is spent at the lower levels so that the students have not had enough time to learn basic facts and ideas, they will become demotivated at the higher levels of the taxonomy as they do not have the required knowledge to make connections.

Put simply the students need to know fundamental facts, ideas and principles in order to have something to think about. These fundamental facts, ideas and principles can be considered as grain that is fed into the mill (the brain) and the resultant flour is used to make a new product called bread (new meanings). So teaching requires a careful balance, with assessment playing an important role in maintaining the appropriate rate of progression. SOLO Taxonomy provides the sequential framework, at the end of which the student can create new meanings for themselves.

Passive and active learning

SOLO Taxonomy can also help to predict if students will be passive or active in their involvement in learning. Passive learning requires students to do no or little processing of or thinking about information presented to them. The students are simply seen as the recipients of information; they might be involved in activities such as copying notes or watching a video after which they would only be expected to recall facts. In teaching science it is too easy to fall into the routine of simply transmitting facts, ideas or principles to the students because of time (or examination) constraints. In terms of SOLO Taxonomy, in such circumstances the students would only be working at the unistructural and multistructural levels, which potentially can lead them to disengage because the work is not challenging enough.

Active learning allows the students to participate in the learning process and challenges them to make new meanings. Activities at the relational or extended abstract level of the taxonomy promote active learning. Critically, such activities depend on surface knowledge so the optimal approach is to develop surface knowledge that then leads to these activities. Too often, activity-based teaching and learning that have no foundation in surface knowledge are ineffective and disengaging.

Using SOLO Taxonomy to construct a learning log

In this book SOLO Taxonomy has been used to develop a learning log. A learning log simply breaks down a series of learning intentions under three levels of SOLO:

1. uni/multistructural – combining the unistructural and multistructural levels for the learning intentions and success criteria, as they are closely related

2. relational

3. extended abstract.

For simplicity, the prestructural level (at which competence has not been achieved) has been removed altogether. Example 2 below illustrates the general layout of the learning log.

Example 2: Excerpt from a learning log

Learning intentions	
SLO 1: *The particles that make up matter are made up of atoms, and some particles are atoms and some are molecules.*	
Uni/multistructural	Be able to define atoms, elements and molecules.
Relational	Be able to explain that atoms do not normally occur individually and they are more commonly found in molecules.
Extended abstract	Be able to make a prediction about the future number of elements.
Learning intentions	
SLO 2: *We represent elements with symbols.*	
Uni/multistructural	Be able to list numerous elements with their correct symbols.
Relational	Be able to classify elements as metals and non-metals.
Extended abstract	Be able to make a generalisation about one aspect of metals and non-metals.

The learning log is the entry into understanding how SOLO Taxonomy works through a simple process of aligning the levels of thinking with what a teacher wants their students to achieve. John Biggs calls this process **constructive alignment**. It is a process that is appropriate for all age groups and subjects. To provide a tangible illustration of the far-reaching potential of this model, this book focuses on science at primary and secondary school levels.

1. Getting started

In this section you will learn about the first steps involved in using SOLO Taxonomy to:

☐ identify and classify relevant facts, ideas and concepts

☐ sequence them into a clear order

☐ identify contexts that can be used to extend the students' thinking on a topic being studied.

Table 1 provides of an overview of the phases and steps involved in this process.

Table 1: Overview of using SOLO to construct a unit of work

Step number	Description
Phase One	
1	*Identify all facts, ideas and concepts that are related to the content you wish to teach.* This is a simple process that only requires the collation of terms related to the topic being taught. It can be done with a mind map.
2	*Classify all facts, ideas and concepts into the appropriate levels of SOLO Taxonomy.* Identifying the basic facts and ideas that fit into the uni/multistructural level is quite straightforward. In the relational level, look for processes or concepts that need to be explained by linking ideas or facts. There will be few if any contexts suitable for extended abstract at this step.
3	*Identify possible contexts that can be used to extend the students' thinking and can be classified at the extended abstract level.* The extended abstract level is the most challenging of the levels to find suitable contexts for. You might search the internet for applications of the topic you are preparing for, or visit websites containing the latest science news for sources of inspiration. Also make use of colleagues and discuss your ideas and thoughts.
Phase Two	
1	*Group key facts, ideas, concepts and possible contexts.* After identifying the key facts, ideas, concepts and new contexts, it is important to start making the connections between them in order to start forming learning intentions.
2	*Assign the verbs of SOLO.* Choose the verbs in SOLO Taxonomy that are linked to levels of thinking or outcomes that you wish to observe in students.
Phase Three	
1	Create challenging learning intentions.
2	Create appropriate success criteria.

The process summarised in Table 1 has been used to develop two exemplars, one for an upper primary school and the other for a secondary school. The following pages take you through the first two phases of the process; Phase Three, when you create learning intentions and success criteria, is covered in the next section. Regardless of your own level of teaching, it is helpful to study both exemplars as they highlight how SOLO Taxonomy can be used at differing levels of complexity depending on the age and level of development of the students. In other words the complexity of thinking expected of a 10-year-old is going to be quite different from that expected of a 15-year-old.

Exemplar: Constructing a unit of work at the primary school level

Example 3 that follows takes you through the first two phases of using SOLO Taxonomy to construct a unit of work for a Year 5/6 science class.

After grouping the key facts, ideas, processes and new contexts in Phase Two, it is possible to assign the verbs from the appropriate level of SOLO Taxonomy according to the outcome you want to achieve. Example 4 combines information from Steps 1 and 2 of Phase Two. It shows the different ways in which verbs from SOLO Taxonomy can be aligned with the content from each SOLO level. Initially more than one verb may be appropriate; later the number will be reduced in the process of constructing the learning intentions and the success criteria (see Section 2).

Example 3: Constructing a unit of work for a Year 5/6 science class

Year level: 5/6	Topic: Electricity and magnetism		
Phase One			
Step 1: Identify all facts, ideas and concepts that are related to the content you wish to teach.			
Electricity	Parallel circuit	Open circuit	Sound
Transformed	Conductor	Circuit diagram	Heat
Poles	Mains	Circuit	Chemical
Electrons	Series circuit	Closed circuit	Electrical
Magnetism	Insulator	Alternative energy	Nuclear
Atom	Batteries	Energy	Kinetic
Magnet	Switch	Current	Potential
Static electricity	Electrical grid	Saving energy	Electromagnets
Electric charge	Cells	Transmitted	Transfer
Negative	Lamp	Magnetic field	Volts
Current electricity	Appliance	Importance of electricity	Amps
Magnetic	Wire	Light	Watts
Positive			

Step 2: Classify all facts, ideas and concepts into the appropriate levels of SOLO Taxonomy.		
Uni/multistructural	Relational	Extended abstract
Current	Current electricity	Electrical grid
Cells	Static electricity	Energy
Batteries	Magnetic field	Alternative energy
Wire	Transformed	Saving energy
Circuit	Transmitted	Importance of electricity
Positive	Magnetic	Electromagnets
Negative	Conductor	
Poles	Insulator	
Appliance		
Lamp		
Switch		
Atom		

continued ...

Example 3: Constructing a unit of work for a Year 5/6 science class (continued)

Step 3: Identify possible contexts that can be used to extend the students' thinking and can be classified at the extended abstract level.

Possible context	Reference or source
Alternative energy	www.hi-energy.org.uk/Education/Primary-School-Factsheets.htm
Saving electricity	http://library.thinkquest.org/06aug/00442/homeelectricity.htm
Importance of electricity	www.watersheds.org/education/gstudent.htm

Phase Two

Step 1: Group key facts, ideas, concepts and possible contexts.

Uni/multistructural		Relational	Extended abstract
Energy Electrical Chemical Nuclear	Sound Light Kinetic Potential	Transfer Transformation	Energy and fossil fuels Saving energy Alternative energy
Electricity Appliance Transmitted		Current electricity Static electricity	Importance of electricity in our everyday lives Electrical grid
Circuits Parallel Series Lamp Wires Switch Open and closed circuits	Current Batteries Circuit diagram Negative Positive	Complete and incomplete circuits Series and parallel circuits	Create own device using a circuit
Volts Amps Watts		Flow of electrons and measuring amperes Volts and effect on brightness of lamps Watts and light bulbs	Appliances used at home Differences in amps, volts and watts
Conductor Insulator Electrons		Classifying objects as insulators or conductors	Uses of insulators and conductors
Magnets Magnetism Magnetic field Poles		Magnetic	Value of magnetism
Electromagnets Current Electrons		Conductor Amps	Strength of magnets

continued ...

Example 3: Constructing a unit of work for a Year 5/6 science class (continued)

Step 2: Assign the verbs of SOLO.		
Uni/multistructural	Relational	Extended abstract
Describe Identify Name List Follow a simple procedure	Compare and contrast Explain causes Sequence Analyse Relate Form an analogy Apply Criticise Justify	Evaluate Theorise Predict Hypothesise Reflect Generate Formulate

Example 4: Assigning verbs to the intended learning outcome for a Year 5/6 science class

Learning outcome	SOLO level				
	Uni/multistructural		Relational	Extended abstract	
Outcome A					
Content	Energy Electrical Chemical Nuclear	Sound Light Kinetic Potential	Transfer Transformation	Energy and fossil fuels Saving energy Alternative energy	
Verb(s)	Identify List	Define Describe	Compare and contrast	Reflect Predict	
Outcome B					
Content	Electricity Appliance Transmitted		Current electricity Static electricity	Importance of electricity in our everyday lives Electrical grid	
Verb(s)	Define Describe		Compare and contrast	Reflect	
Outcome C					
Content	Circuits Parallel Series Lamp Wires Switch Open and closed circuits	Current Batteries Circuit diagram Negative Positive	Complete and incomplete circuits Series and parallel circuits	Create own device using a circuit	
Verb(s)	Define Identify Describe		Relate	Create	

Exemplar: Constructing a unit of work at the secondary school level

Example 5 takes you through the first two phases of using SOLO Taxonomy to construct a unit of work for a Year 9/10 physics class.

Example 6 then shows the different ways in which verbs from the SOLO Taxonomy can be aligned with the content from each SOLO level, as identified in Step 1 of Phase Two.

Example 5: Constructing a unit of work for a Year 9/10 physics class

Year level: 9/10		Topic: Light	
Phase One			
Step 1: Identify all facts, ideas and concepts that are related to the content you wish to teach.			
Law of reflection	Normal	Transparent	Long-sighted
Mirror	Refraction	Medium	Energy
Spectrum	Light ray	Retina	Focal point
Cornea	Dispersion	Refractor	Prism
Image	Diverging	Cone cells	Plane surface
Rainbow	Concave	Rod cells	Transformation
Incident	Convex	Focus	Material
Converging	Lens	Short-sighted	Translucent
Inverted			

Step 2: Classify all facts, ideas and concepts into the appropriate levels of SOLO Taxonomy.

Uni/multistructural	Relational	Extended abstract
Mirror	Law of reflection	Energy
Rainbow	Diverging	
Normal	Dispersion	
Medium	Spectrum	
Focal point	Refraction	
Object	Converging	
Transparent	Short-sighted	
Prism	Long-sighted	
Cone cells		
Plane surface		

Step 3: Identify contexts that can be used to extend the students' thinking and can be classified at the extended abstract level.

Possible contexts	Reference or source
Glass that only allows light to pass one way	www.wired.com/wiredscience/2011/04/one-way-light
Light and microscopes	www.forensicscience.org/resources/light-microscope
How light moves molecules	esciencenews.com/articles/2011/03/16/hopkins.researchers.use.light.move.molecules

continued ...

Example 5: Constructing a unit of work for a Year 9/10 physics class (continued)

Phase Two		
Step 1: Group key facts, ideas, concepts and possible contexts.		
Uni/multistructural	Relational	Extended abstract
Light Energy Light travels in straight lines Speed of light	Light can be transformed into other forms of energy	Light and its importance to communication
Normal Plane surface Angle of reflection Angle of incidence Reflection Incidence Ray Ray diagram	Law of reflection	Law of reflection on all rough and smooth surfaces
Concave mirror Convex mirror Focal point Convergent Divergent	Behaviour of light in concave and convex mirrors	How image changes in a concave mirror depending on the focal distance
Object Reflect Refract Medium Material Opaque Transparent Translucent	Behaviour of light passing though different media	Speed of light through different media
Refraction Refractor Parallel Rays Concave Convex	Uses of refractors	Generalised statement about behaviour of parallel rays
Step 2: Assign the verbs of SOLO. Categorise the verbs from SOLO Taxonomy against the content at the uni/multistructural, relational and extended abstract levels (see Example 6 that follows).		

Example 6: Assigning verbs to the intended learning outcome for a Year 9/10 physics class

Learning outcome	SOLO level		
	Uni/multistructural	Relational	Extended abstract
Outcome A			
Facts, ideas, processes and context	Light Energy Light travels in straight lines Speed of light	Light can be transformed into other forms of energy	Light and its importance to medicine and communication
Verb(s)	Define Identify	Explain	Reflect
Outcome B			
Facts, ideas, processes and context	Rays Ray diagram Normal Angle of reflection Angle of incidence Plane surface	Law of reflection	Is law of reflection true for all surfaces?
Verb(s)	Define Describe	Relate	Predict Hypothesise
Outcome C			
Facts, ideas, processes and context	Mirror Concave mirror Convex mirror Focal point Parallel rays	Distance of object from mirror	Generalisation of concave and convex mirrors
Verb(s)	Define Describe	Relate	Generalise

Concave mirror
Convex mirror

Distance of object from mirror

Generalisation of concave and convex mirrors

A practical guide to constructing a unit of work

Template 1 below shows how you can construct an entire unit of work following the same process as outlined in the previous exemplars. Note that at this stage the groups you have formed do not have to be in any logical order. The sequencing of these groups will be explained in the next section.

Template 1: Using SOLO to construct a unit of work

	Uni/multistructural	Relational	Extended abstract
Group 1 Facts, ideas, processes and context			
SOLO verb(s)			
Group 2 Facts, ideas, processes and context			
SOLO verb(s)			
Group 3 Facts, ideas, processes and context			
SOLO verb(s)			
Group 4 Facts, ideas, processes and context			
SOLO verb(s)			
Group 5 Facts, ideas, processes and context			
SOLO verb(s)			
Group 6 Facts, ideas, processes and context			
SOLO verb(s)			
Group 7 Facts, ideas, processes and context			
SOLO verb(s)			

Now that the verbs have been assigned, a framework has developed. In the next section we look at how we can use this framework to design the appropriate teaching activities or interventions for each level of SOLO Taxonomy.

2. Putting it all together

In Phase Three of the process outlined in Table 1 (see Section 1), the learning intentions and success criteria can be constructed. Both these components will be important in providing clarity throughout a unit of work or during any teaching interaction. They form the foundation from which teachers know what they want the learning to look like and at the same time they provide students with a clear path to follow in order to achieve identified outcomes.

Success criteria from a student's perspective

In this process, each learning intention is broken down into a corresponding success criterion. The success criteria have a very important role when you are using the learning log. Notably they make clear to the student how the student is doing in relation to the learning intention. Once the student has ascertained "where they are" using the success criteria, they can establish (in collaboration with the teacher) what they need to do next. The criteria become the focus of discussions and provide valuable information to the student and teacher on the student's progress at the differing levels of thinking.

The success criteria are designed from a student's perspective because they provide students with the opportunity to evaluate how effectively they are working. In this way students can:

☐ monitor their own progress and reflect on the level of success they have had

☐ develop a much better idea of their own ability and thus build the foundation on which they can direct their own learning.

Many success criteria written from a teacher's perspective do not use language that students can understand easily. As a result, students may not know what they have to do in order to be successful. Likewise, if teachers use tests to evaluate whether students have achieved the success criteria, the students gain little information as to why they were successful or not. In addition, in contrast to providing the success criteria within the learning log, this approach does not allow students to direct their own learning.

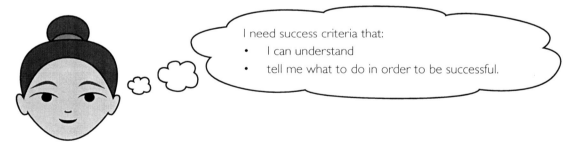

I need success criteria that:
• I can understand
• tell me what to do in order to be successful.

Sequencing groups and developing learning intentions and success criteria

In the first two phases of the process covered in Section 1, facts, ideas, processes and contexts were organised into groups, and sample verbs from SOLO Taxonomy were assigned to the appropriate levels for two exemplars (primary and secondary school levels). You need to sequence these groups into a logical order through which you want the students to progress. It is important to consider factors such as:

☐ natural links between groups

☐ prior knowledge of students

☐ level of complexity.

To produce a unit of work from the groups that you have identified, you then need to create a learning intention and success criterion for each level of SOLO Taxonomy for each of the groups. Examples 7 and 8 that follow show this process for one group from the primary exemplar and another from the secondary exemplar described in Section 1.

Example 7: Developing learning intentions and success criteria for a Year 5/6 science class

Component	SOLO level		
	Uni/multistructural	Relational	Extended abstract
Content	Energy Electrical Chemical Nuclear Sound Light Kinetic Potential	Transfer Transformation	Energy and fossil fuels Saving energy Alternative energy
Verb(s)	Identify List Define Describe	Compare and contrast	Reflect Predict
Learning intention	Be able to identify the many forms of energy.	Be able to compare and contrast the terms *energy transfer* and *transformation*.	Be able to reflect on the benefits of saving energy.
Success criterion	I can identify the various forms of energy.	I can identify the similarities and differences between energy transfer and transformation.	I can reflect on how I can save energy and the benefits this brings.

Example 8: Developing learning intentions and success criteria for a Year 9/10 physics class

Component	SOLO level		
	Uni/multistructural	Relational	Extended abstract
Facts, ideas, processes and context	Light Energy Light travels in straight lines Speed of light	Light can be transformed into other forms of energy	Light and its importance to medicine and communication
Verb(s)	Define Identify	Explain	Reflect
Learning intention	Be able to define the terms *light* and *energy*, and identify some properties of light.	Know that light can be transformed into other forms of energy.	Be able to reflect on the importance of light in medicine and communication.
Success criterion/criteria	I can define the terms *light* and *energy*. I can identify some properties of light.	I can explain how light is transformed into other types of energy.	I can reflect on the importance of light in medicine and communication

Learning log exemplars

When you have completed this process for all the groups and sequenced them logically, you have created a learning log that differentiates learning intentions and success criteria under three levels of SOLO Taxonomy. The first completed learning log that follows is appropriate for the primary level (Example 9) and the second one for the secondary level (Example 10).

Example 9: Learning log for a Year 5/6 science class

SOLO level	Learning intentions	Success criteria
Generalised learning intention: Understand energy has many forms and that it can be transferred and transformed.		
Uni/multistructural	Be able to identify the different forms of energy.	I can identify the various forms of energy.
Relational	Be able to compare and contrast the terms *energy transfer* and *transformation*.	I can identify the similarities and differences between energy transfer and transformation.
Extended abstract	Be able to reflect on the benefits of saving energy.	I can reflect on how I can save energy and the benefits this brings.
Generalised learning intention: Understand that electricity has two forms and its impact on our everyday lives.		
Uni/multistructural	Be able to define current and static electricity.	I can define current and static electricity.
Relational	Be able to contrast current and static electricity and explain how electricity reaches our homes.	I can identify the differences between current and static electricity and explain how electricity reaches our homes via the national electricity grid.
Extended abstract	Be able to predict the absence of electricity on our lives.	I can predict how having no electricity would affect our lives.
Generalised learning intention: Understand how circuits are constructed and that appliances are represented by symbols.		
Uni/multistructural	Be able to follow simple instructions and diagrams in building complete circuits and understand that electricity is the flow of electrons.	I can follow simple instructions using diagrams to build complete circuits. I can describe electricity in terms of electrons.
Relational	Be able to explain why electrons can flow in a complete circuit but not in an incomplete (broken) circuit.	I can explain, in relation to electrons, the difference between complete and incomplete circuits.
Extended abstract	Be able to create own circuit using a variety of appliances.	I can create my own circuit using a variety of appliances.
Generalised learning intention: Understand the similarities and differences between series and parallel circuits.		
Uni/multistructural	Be able to define series and parallel circuits.	I can define series and parallel circuits.
Relational	Be able to compare and contrast series and parallel circuits.	I can identify the similarities and differences between series and parallel circuits.
Extended abstract	Be able to predict the best situation in which to use series and parallel circuits.	I can predict the best applications of series and parallel circuits.

continued ...

Example 9: Learning log for a Year 5/6 science class (continued)

SOLO level	Learning intentions	Success criteria
Generalised learning intention: Understand the relationship between volts, amps and watts.		
Uni/multistructural	Be able to define the terms *volts*, *amps* and *watts*.	I can define the terms *volts*, *amps* and *watts*.
Relational	Be able to explain the effect of varying volts, amps and watts on the brightness of a lamp.	I can explain the effect of varying the volts, amps and watts on the brightness of a lamp.
Extended abstract	Be able to reflect on how common appliances are designed to use appropriate volts, amps and watts.	I can reflect on how volts, amps and watts are used differently on various appliances.
Generalised learning intention: Understand how objects can be conductors and insulators.		
Uni/multistructural	Be able to define the terms *conductors* and *insulators*.	I can define the terms *conductors* and *insulators*.
Relational	Be able to classify objects as conductors and insulators.	I can classify various objects as conductors and insulators.
Extended abstract	Be able to predict the uses of electrical conductors and insulators.	I can predict the uses of electrical conductors and insulators.
Generalised learning intention: Understand that magnets have a magnetic field.		
Uni/multistructural	Be able to define the terms *magnet*, *magnetism*, *magnetic field* and *poles*.	I can define the terms *magnet*, *magnetism*, *magnetic field* and *poles*.
Relational	Be able to relate the strength of a magnet to the size of its magnetic field.	I can relate the strength of a magnet to the size of its magnetic field.
Extended abstract	Be able to create an experiment to test the strength of magnets.	I can create an experiment that tests the strength of magnets.
Generalised learning intention: Understand how electromagnets are temporary magnets.		
Uni/multistructural	Be able to define the term *electromagnet*.	I can define the term *electromagnet*.
Relational	Be able to explain how electromagnets are made.	I can explain how electromagnets are made.
Extended abstract	Be able to hypothesise about how the strength of electromagnets can be changed.	I can hypothesise about how the strength of electromagnets can be changed.

Example 10: Learning log for a Year 9/10 physics class

SOLO level	Learning intentions	Success criteria
Generalised learning intention: Recognise that light and sound are types of energy that are detected by eyes and ears.		
Uni/multistructural	Be able to define the terms *light* and *energy* and identify some properties of light.	I can define the terms *light* and *energy*. I can identify some properties of light .
Relational	Know that light can be transformed into other forms of energy.	I can explain how light is transformed into other types of energy.
Extended abstract	Be able to reflect on the importance of light in medicine and communication.	I can reflect on the importance of light in medicine and communication.
Generalised learning intention: Be able to draw a normal, measure angles and define the law of reflection.		
Uni/multistructural	Be able to draw ray diagrams including the normal with correctly drawn angles.	I can draw a ray diagram with correctly measured angles.
Relational	Be able to define the law of reflection, relating the terms *incidence, reflected ray, normal* and *smooth surface*.	I can define the law of reflection, relating the terms *incidence, reflected ray, normal* and *smooth surface*.
Extended abstract	Recognise that the law of reflection is true for all plane surfaces and be able to predict what will happen if the surface is rough.	I can predict what will happen if light is reflected off a rough surface and explain why it happens.
Generalised learning intention: Be able to use ray boxes to understand how concave and convex mirrors behave.		
Uni/multistructural	Know that changing the distance of an object from a concave mirror changes the appearance of the image.	I can recognise that an image in a concave mirror changes as an object is moved closer or further away from the mirror.
Relational	Be able to explain why concave mirrors are known as *converging mirrors* and convex mirrors as *diverging mirrors*.	I can (using diagrams) explain why concave and convex mirrors are referred to as *convergent* and *divergent mirrors* respectively.
Extended abstract	Recognise patterns in reflected rays from concave and convex mirrors and be able to make a generalisation.	I can write a generalisation about the patterns of reflected rays in concave and convex mirrors.
Generalised learning intention: Know that shiny objects reflect light and transparent objects refract light.		
Uni/multistructural	Recognise that shiny objects reflect light and transparent objects refract it.	I can recognise the types of materials that reflect light and those that will allow light to pass through them.
Relational	Be able to explain why light can pass through some materials and not others.	I can explain why light refracts in materials through which it passes.
Extended abstract	Predict what will happen to the speed of light in different media using an analogy.	I can predict what will happen to the speed of light in different media using an analogy.
Generalised learning intention: Understand how refraction is influenced by the refractor.		
Uni/multistructural	Be able to draw the refracted rays when passing through a concave and convex refractor.	I can draw lines that represent refracted rays when they have passed through a concave and convex refractor.

continued ...

Example 10: Learning log for a Year 9/10 physics class (continued)

SOLO level	Learning intentions	Success criteria
Relational	Be able to relate the properties of concave and convex refractors to their uses.	I can relate the properties of concave and convex refractors to their uses.
Extended abstract	Be able to write a generalisation about the behaviour of parallel rays in concave and convex refractors.	I can write a generalisation about the behaviour of parallel rays in concave and convex refractors.
Generalised learning intention: Be able to classify various reflectors and refractors.		
Uni/multistructural	Be able to classify several reflectors and refractors into three groups: plane, concave and convex.	I can correctly organise several reflectors and refractors into these groups: plane, concave and convex.
Relational	Be able to explain why several refractors and reflectors can be considered plane, concave and convex.	I can explain why each of the reflectors and refractors was placed in its particular group.
Extended abstract	Be able to create a way to test grouped refractors and reflectors to ensure they are placed in the correct groups.	I can create a way to test whether each reflector and refractor has been placed in the correct group.
Generalised learning intention: Be able to describe the function of refractors in various devices.		
Uni/multistructural	Be able to identify the refractor in a cow's eye.	I can identify the refractor in a cow's eye.
Relational	Be able to explain how the refractor in a cow's eye focuses the light rays on the retina.	I can explain how the refractor length affects the length at which the rays are focused.
Extended abstract	Be able to predict the effects of a cow's refractor that does not work correctly.	I can predict what will happen if the refractor is too short or too long on the focal point of the rays.
Generalised learning intention: Be able to define long- and short-sightedness.		
Uni/multistructural	Be able to identify the ray diagram that shows long- and short-sightedness.	I can identify long- and short-sightedness by using ray diagrams.
Relational	Be able to explain, in terms of the refractor, why somebody can be long- or short-sighted.	I can explain how a refractor that is too short or too long affects sight.
Extended abstract	Be able to predict the type of lens that could be used to correct long- or short-sightedness.	I can predict which type of lens will correct long-sightedness and which type will correct short-sightedness.
Generalised learning intention: Know how white light is dispersed and how rainbows are formed.		
Uni/multistructural	Be able to define the term *spectrum* and remember the mnemonic *ROYGBIV*.	I can define the term *spectrum*.
Relational	Be able to explain how light is dispersed into a spectrum and relate this to the formation of rainbows.	I can explain how light is dispersed using a prism and relate this to how rainbows are formed in the atmosphere.
Extended abstract	Be able to make a generalisation about the quality of a rainbow.	I can form a generalisation about the formation of spectrums and rainbows in relation to the amount of refraction occurring.

3. The pedagogy behind the learning log

Science is a subject that contains not only a large amount of new ideas and information, but also a large number of abstract ideas which can be daunting and inaccessible to many students. These characteristics can undermine students' motivation, leading them to consider that they are no good at science (and to withdraw from the subject as soon as they can).

Although many struggle with learning the numerous surface-level notions, there are also many students who can understand the more complex abstract ideas but never have the opportunity to apply them in a wider context or use their imagination or creativity to generate new ideas of their own. Because of this lack of opportunity, they too can fail to engage in the subject.

The learning log is a framework that can be used to both make science accessible to students and provide them with opportunities to create their own ideas through the use of higher-order thinking. With reference to the success criteria, it can also be used to assess where individual students are along a continuum from surface to deep thinking. This information can be invaluable for the teacher in evaluating the impact of their teaching.

This section explores in more detail the pedagogical rationale that underpins the learning log and, in doing so, provides insight into how and why it can be used so effectively in the classroom.

Providing clarity in teaching and learning

A single learning intention that a teacher provides to students can be interpreted in many different ways. It is more than likely that it will not identify the key terms, ideas or concepts that need to be taught or learnt to meet the specified learning intention and that it will not necessarily sequence these in terms of complexity or cognitive activity. A teacher may well plan their lesson taking all these factors into consideration but such factors will not be clear or visible to the student.

In contrast, the learning log provides clarity to the teacher and student as it:

☐ specifies clearly the intended outcomes that require different levels of thinking

☐ sequences them hierarchically.

To the student, the learning log can then show a clear pathway that states what is expected in terms of content and the thinking skills that they will be required to use.

The learning intentions in the learning log provide a framework against which the teacher and student can assess how well the student meets a learning intention, with reference to the success criteria. This information can be valuable to both teacher and student in determining the level of complexity that a student can work at successfully.

Accessibility to all students

The learning log at the unistructural and multistructural levels identifies learning intentions that require little cognitive activity as they generally involve activities concerned with listing, defining or describing. All students can complete such activities, with varying degrees of support. This experience is especially important for those students who have little confidence in their own ability as it shows them that they can achieve an identified learning outcome and it is an important step in improving their self efficacy (Figure 2). In many cases it is also critical that students have these surface-level notions before they can go on to relate and extend them further.

Figure 2: Completing unistructural and multistructural activities can lift self efficacy

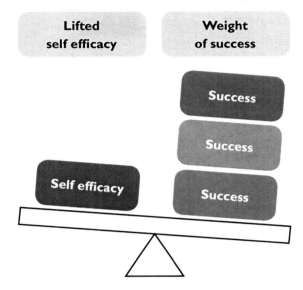

Providing challenging learning intentions for all students

Where a teacher uses a single learning intention, a student may perceive it as either too hard or too easy and become demotivated as a result. Likewise, within any classroom there will be students who will be challenged by a learning intention aimed at surface learning while others will achieve it comfortably and require further opportunities to test their understanding. With its three levels of learning intentions and thus three levels of cognitive complexity, the learning log provides a progression in the complexity of challenge to all students in the classroom. It is more likely to provide a challenge to all students and maintain their engagement in what is being taught.

I will illustrate this consequence with reference to two Year 10 students from a mainstream science class, who I have observed from my own experience in the classroom while using the learning log.

Student A: Seizing the opportunity to succeed

Student A is a boy who had been transferred into my class after about a term with another teacher. I am not aware of the reasons for the move but he came with a reputation for misbehaviour and a poor attitude towards his work. These traits became evident quite quickly but I had a sense there was more to him than his demonstrable attitude indicated.

After a few lessons we started a new topic where I took the opportunity to explain what the learning log was and how it worked. Initially, his attitude did not show any change but I sat with him and assisted him in his effort at the first of the learning intentions at the unistructural and multistructural level. At first he was hesitant to attempt the work but soon discovered that he was capable of doing the work and could meet the success criteria. The look on his face when he realised that he could do it was one of surprise and pride. He attempted the next learning intention at the unistructural and multistructural level on his own and again he was successful.

His attitude to his work began to change and although he is now not working at a high level he is putting effort into his work. The next challenge for him will be to attempt a learning intention identified at the relational level.

Student B: Rising to the challenge

Student B is a girl who demonstrated she had an interest and a good ability in science. However, she was often off-task and distracted others in their learning. When I introduced the learning log, her attitude changed visibly.

I sat down with her and questioned her about the change in her behaviour. She stated that prior to the learning log she was bored and found the work too easy so she accepted that she would not place extra effort into thinking about whatever was being studied. We reflected on the learning intentions that I gave prior to the learning log and now viewed them as being too simplistic and aimed at low levels of thinking; once she felt that she had met the criteria for these intentions, she had no challenge. However with the learning log now identifying learning intentions with ever-increasing demands on cognitive activity, the challenge had returned for her.

Student B stated, "My goal for each lesson is to meet the success criteria for all levels of the learning log."

These are just two examples of experiences that made me fully appreciate the value of the learning log in providing challenge to students no matter what their ability is. They also demonstrate how a teacher can use the learning log to place each student relative to their understanding and then move them forward towards the success criteria. I carefully reviewed the intentions I had incorporated into the learning log with a specific focus on the level of challenge they provided. If the intentions at each level were too easy or too hard, a student might disengage from the work. For the balance to be right, the intentions must give the student a chance to succeed but at the same time there must be a chance of failure: only in this situation would a student feel there was sufficient but not insurmountable challenge. It is also important to show a student what success will look like as they progress through the learning log, so that they can appreciate a sense of mastery as they invest more effort and practice in meeting the success criteria.

An important question I also considered was, "What would motivate a student to attempt a learning intention within the learning log if they had not been successful the first time?" Through observations in the classroom I came to the conclusion that they would make another attempt if they felt there was a greater chance of success after feedback from either myself or other students. This observation highlighted the value of prompt feedback.

Encouraging intrinsic motivation

Intrinsic motivation comes from within a person and relies on no external source of reward or recognition. I have heard the advice "Do the best you can do" and "Don't compare yourself with anybody else" many times over the years and have only linked it recently to the idea of intrinsic motivation. These fatherly statements focus the attention on what an individual can control rather than on what they cannot. It puts the emphasis on the satisfaction an individual gets when they make personal progress by achieving something new. The feeling is deeply personal and can be undermined when the achievement is compared with what others have done because there will always be somebody who can do it faster and easier. Without this internal sense of satisfaction, motivation for trying tasks can dwindle.

All students are intrinsically motivated towards some aspect of their life, be it sport, art, building things, or any of a number of academic (or non-academic) subjects. Often they have this motivation because they have had early success in this field, recognise they have some kind of talent with it, and enjoy attempting new tasks that continue to demonstrate this talent. The problem is: how you get them to be intrinsically motivated in science? Through observing my own students I consider there are two key parts to this task:

1. Provide the opportunity to show a student that they have some level of ability or talent in the subject.

2. Focus on the progress each student has made, without comparing it with anybody else.

A cognitive centre

The learning log, including its repetition of the verbs in SOLO Taxonomy, allows the brain to make connections specifically related to the use and development of thinking skills. As with learning any new skill, the learner's first attempts at using a targeted thinking skill are often unsuccessful or below the level the learner wishes to achieve. Yet by practising the skill repeatedly, collecting information on performance and comparing this information with previous attempts, the learner can modify new attempts at the skill.

Michael Merzenich suggests that the human brain develops specific centres to process skills like those identified in SOLO Taxonomy. The learning log places these in a context that the learner can identify as important to the way they think and learn and helps establish thinking as culture within the classroom. The repetition in the learning log allows the development of the processing skills related to the verbs in SOLO Taxonomy (Figure 3).

Figure 3: Developing a cognitive processing centre through repetition of SOLO verbs in the learning log

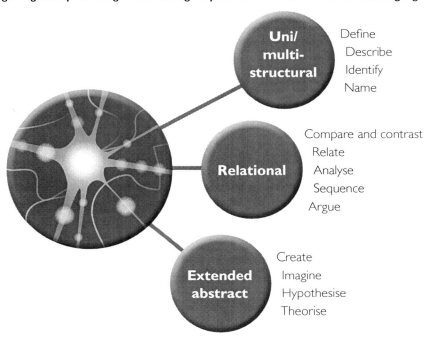

In helping to develop a cognitive centre for processing the skills identified in SOLO Taxonomy, teachers should value repeated opportunities to learn as an important part of the process of improving a skill. In sport, most learners would not hesitate to try a skill in a different way to see if it improved the outcome. If it does not improve the outcome, then the learner may consider there has been an error somewhere in its execution. Such deliberate practice is typically necessary in learning most tasks (which, in addition to sport, may range from music to socially unacceptable tasks such as stealing). Reflection on the skill could help identify where the error occurred and guide the learner in modifying their next approach.

In a classroom context my experience suggests that students are far more reticent to take the risk of deliberate practice as they tend to consider an error as failure and this view has the potential to reduce a student's self efficacy and therefore willingness to make another attempt. Many of those who struggle and are in most need of deliberate practice try once and then either do not wish to take the risk of re-learning in case they fail the second time or see that they have put in their "best effort" even if the answer is incorrect. In developing students' ability to take risks with their thinking, it is essential to take time to highlight that:

☐ the process of trial and error is an important part of learning

☐ an error is not the same as failure.

Too often students do not want to share their ideas or thinking, as they consider a wrong answer would mean their peers would see them as a failure. In students who are academically able this is still a barrier as they do not want to risk their reputation on an answer they do not know is completely correct.

And a major concern is the negative claims, comments, vibes from their peers – this is a powerful detriment. We ignore the power of peers at our peril.

Self managing

The learning log provides a framework from which students can learn to self-regulate; that is, to control monitoring, evaluating and planning their own learning. The initial shift – and a very important one that is often hard to achieve – is for a student to focus on their own performance. Too often in many classrooms, students achieve this focus by comparing their performance with that of their peers; for effective self-management, however, the aim should be that they spend cognitive energy comparing and analysing different aspects of their own performance. Unpacking the SOLO Taxonomy levels in the learning log allows individual students to focus on the thinking skills, strategies and behaviours that can improve their own performance (Figure 4) and to monitor their own progress at each of these hierarchical levels. The log provides a rubric that helps them to:

☐ monitor what they need to do

☐ recognise what success looks like

☐ gain direction as to where to go next.

They can then reflect on their behaviours and strategies that have led to their success.

In my own classroom I have observed students who were frequently off-task because they considered themselves not to be smart, often because of peer comparison, but once I introduced the learning logs and assisted them with simple strategies that allowed them to achieve success, their behaviour began to change. The students learnt how these new strategies and behaviours could help them to succeed even at a low level of thinking and they proactively applied them in other similar situations. Thus learning becomes more personal in terms of the efficiency and speed at which students travel through the lesson, and ensures all students are working towards similar content and understanding goals.

The same principle applies to gifted or very capable students who have always used their natural ability to get through. When they come up against something they cannot do, they are just as helpless as somebody who is working at a lower level of thinking. They too need help to develop strategies or behaviours that they can redeploy to move towards meeting the success criteria.

Figure 4: Focusing on personal performance as a way of learning to self-regulate

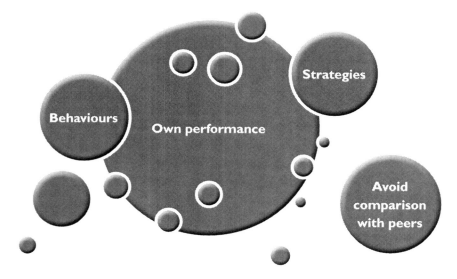

The learning log thus allows students to accumulate strategies and behaviours and to predict when they can use one or more of those strategies and behaviours to increase their chance of success. They are now far more self-regulating and less dependent on others to find ways to enhance their own success.

Differentiation

The learning log provides a personalised framework in the classroom which can allow for differentiation in pace, prior knowledge, the demonstration of student knowledge and the level of challenge.

We all know students are not the same and one of the biggest challenges in the classroom is supporting students so that they feel they have been personally taken into consideration. Each student wants choices and unique opportunities in their own learning. Such inclusion, as the antithesis of the "one size fits all" approach, must surely strengthen students' motivation and engagement.

By way of analogy, think of being at a large conference presentation where all attendees receive the same information, at the same time and in the same format. The attendees cannot choose or control the information they receive; they are simply there to receive it. What happens to those attendees with limited prior knowledge who cannot understand the concepts being presented? They may start wishing they were somewhere else and fortunately for them they can just get up and leave. Equally, for the attendees at the other end of the knowledge and understanding spectrum, the presentation may provide no new information or challenge and that experience, combined with the lack of opportunity for expression, may likewise lead to their disengagement.

Now imagine what would happen if these same attendees had to repeat this situation as frequently as many students in the classroom have to. It is more than likely that they would come to feel that they were not valued and become frustrated through the lack of choice and opportunities. For some students in the equivalent situation, another result is behaviours that are not desired in the classroom.

With the learning log teachers have a tool to leave behind the "one size fits all" approach and embed differentiation in the classroom. For students it creates choice and opportunity, and allows them to work at different paces and levels of thinking. In particular, the learning log:

☐ recognises that students may have different starting places for learning, depending on their prior knowledge, as they work towards the desired goals

☐ offers learning intentions that provide not only different access points for students but also opportunities to demonstrate their competency at each of the SOLO levels

☐ gives students some control over their pace of working, such that some can spend more time as required at the lower levels of thinking while others can progress quickly to the higher levels. Clearly the teacher has an important part in this process as they have to provide guidance and feedback to help students determine the appropriate pace.

For the teacher too there are many benefits arising from the differentiation that can be achieved through identifying the different levels of thinking in the learning log. Among these benefits are that:

☐ the teacher knows that the framework caters for all possible paces of student learning

☐ there is a variety of entry points for students

☐ the progressive framework is visible to students

☐ the teacher is able to support students at a variety of levels.

Importantly the learning log overcomes the need for the teacher to create new activities or issue question numbers from a book just to keep students active – an approach that is reactive and that students know is reactive, which undermines its value. By contrast, students perceive the learning log as an authentic and integral programme for their learning.

Formative interpretations

Making formative interpretations from assessment is one of the most powerful tools available to teachers and students and should happen frequently in a classroom. It has a significant influence on the development of students' knowledge and the way a teacher presents information. In formative assessment:

☐ students are not given grades or scores but rather gain information that can improve their performance in a particular skill or activity

☐ teachers can learn much about the impact of their teaching (and obviously much more than they would if the students gave them only a grade or score!).

The process therefore is reciprocal as both teacher and students learn from formative interpretations, and their future actions are influenced by the information they gain from it (Figure 5).

Figure 5: The reciprocal process of making formative interpretations

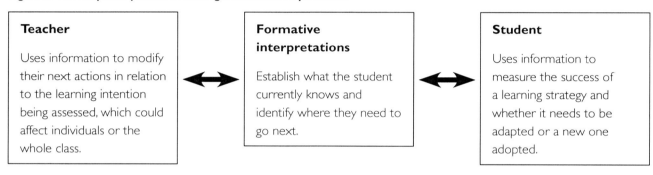

Teacher	Formative interpretations	Student
Uses information to modify their next actions in relation to the learning intention being assessed, which could affect individuals or the whole class.	Establish what the student currently knows and identify where they need to go next.	Uses information to measure the success of a learning strategy and whether it needs to be adapted or a new one adopted.

As well as providing different learning intentions to be formatively evaluated, the learning log establishes the basis of strategies that the students can use at each of those levels. It provides the teacher with a clear focus in terms of the questions they pose or evidence they are looking for in order to assess each student's performance accurately. Formative interpretations are most beneficial when they are immediate and focused strongly on "where to next" – a major advantage of the learning log. They are personal to students and a positive way for teachers to demonstrate their interest in their students' learning.

Students can carry out their own formative interpretations of where they are at in the learning, as the learning log provides the rubric or detailed success criteria. It is a valuable process for them as it is likely to generate questions which they can pose to themselves and to the teacher.

Learning-focused relationships

It is widely accepted that good relationships are important to getting the best out of students. It creates an environment where the interactions are calm, positive and reflective between teachers and students. Achieving good relationships, however, is a challenge that faces any teacher in the classroom because personalities and attitudes of teachers and students are so widely different. Some fundamentals that can be applied effectively to any relationship are:

☐ showing a personal interest in another person, which is often reciprocated

☐ listening carefully to individuals and ensuring that they know they have been heard

☐ being open to the opinions and ideas of others.

Wow! The teacher seems to actually listen to my ideas!

Relationships in the classroom are not exactly the same as those with colleagues and other adults as in classroom relationships the focus is on learning. This means that both teachers and students should make decisions about relationships in the context of learning. It is important for the teacher to be calm and authoritative to set the tone for relationships in a classroom. Students, I believe, are strongly influenced by these qualities, leading them to view the teacher as able to manage interactions in the classroom fairly and competently.

Relationships prosper in a climate of positive reinforcement. We can all think of occasions when we have been praised for a special effort or for an action such as opening a door for someone else. It makes you feel good that you have been noticed and as a result you are likely to repeat that behaviour. It is important to note too that consistent affirmation is more effective than one-off praise. Those individuals who react positively to negative comments are rare.

I would suggest all of us do not receive enough praise for the efforts we make in all aspects of our lives and this is true for students too, but as adults we have learnt to deal with it. Some students may receive no praise from home at all, making the classroom the only place where they may be recognised and rewarded with positive comments.

Student C: Unexpected praise

I heard a story recently that involved a student whose particularly troublesome behaviour, such as sarcastic comments and put-downs, had detrimental effects on many relationships in the classroom. When the teacher made a comment to the boy that acknowledged his obvious intelligence and ability, the reaction was one that the teacher had not anticipated: the boy was open-mouthed in disbelief. Eventually he recovered and replied that he had never been praised like that before in his life. Thereafter the sarcastic comments and put-downs ceased and a relationship developed that was focused purely on learning.

Learning-focused relationships are important because they allow both the student and teacher to reflect on their interactions with a view to how they will improve a student's ability to learn. There is no ambiguity in the purpose of developing good relationships. The learning log helps to establish positive learning relationships as it provides clear opportunities for praise at all levels of thinking. It also uses language that is specific to a student's learning, which encourages both teacher–student and student–student relationships to develop around this commonality of language.

4. The pyramid of a lifelong learner

Schools do not just strive for students to achieve the best they are capable of academically; they also help shape the whole person and prepare them for life after school. The term *lifelong learner* is often used to describe what schools want their students to become and the process of creating a lifelong learner begins as soon as a student begins school. Ideas about what a lifelong learner looks like and what skills they require vary but SOLO Taxonomy and the learning log provide a framework from which to develop such skills. The pyramid of a lifelong learner (Figure 6) proposes the essential elements that are required to become a lifelong learner.

Learning-focused relationships hold the pyramid together in two ways:

1. They deliver and erect the scaffolding, allowing the stones to be placed on top of each other.

2. They provide the mortar that holds the stones together.

Overview of the levels of the pyramid

The cornerstones at the base of the pyramid are **clarity** and **effort**. A student must understand what they are expected to learn and the steps involved in getting there, but must also realise they need to apply effort if they are going to have any success. Persistence, concentration, deliberate practice are taught and learned skills – they need to be explicit and valued, and students are more likely to put in the effort if they are aware of the progression to the success criteria. The learning log is a key feature of this process.

The other foundation stone comprises **choice and opportunities**. There need to be different entry points to the work so that students can choose the one that is appropriate to them. Without such choice, the cornerstone of effort is likely to be weakened.

The following elements are put in place in the next level of stones:

☐ **Formative interpretations** from assessments provide opportunities to identify success for a student and help them understand where they are in the learning log.

☐ A sense of **self efficacy** is strengthened though formative interpretations – students become more confident that they can reach the goals of the lesson. When they feel more positive about themselves, then students will maintain or intensify their effort.

☐ **Challenge** ensures students have something to strive for and, like formative interpretations, encourages the further development of self efficacy.

Using the learning log as a framework for the foundation stones allows a focus on the thinking skills that are required for learning. By practising the identified thinking skills frequently, students can start developing a **cognitive processing centre** and use it to reflect on current and past performance and to modify these skills. As a consequence, they may well increase their chance of success.

Building on from the establishment of a cognitive processing centre, students begin to **self manage** behaviours and strategies they have reflected on as those likely to increase their chance of success. Their **intrinsic motivation** is assisted by their ability to analyse their own progress in relation to a number of thinking skills.

The capstone is the pinnacle of the pyramid, the **lifelong learner** – a student who has the skills and attributes to apply thinking skills, behaviours and strategies to new learning.

Figure 6: Pyramid of a lifelong learner

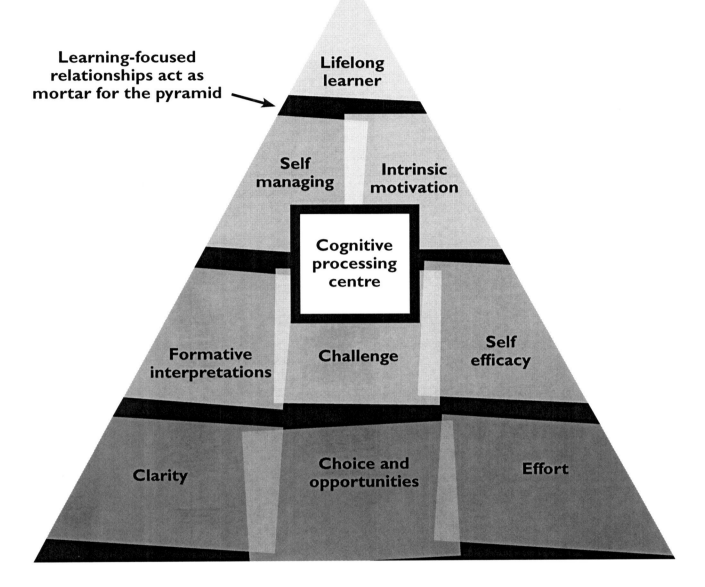

5. Assessing prior knowledge

The prior knowledge students bring into a classroom is unpredictable and varied. If it is not taken into account, it can hinder their learning during a unit of work. Factors that may influence prior knowledge include:

☐ discussions with family members

☐ visits to museums

☐ interest in or passion for a topic.

It is not easy to replace a student's prior knowledge with a new set of information. They need time to compare their existing understanding with new information in order to resolve any contradictions or mismatches by modifying their knowledge. A common example in science is that many students believe the season of summer occurs because the earth is closer to the sun when in fact the real reason is connected to the tilt of the earth and the concentration of rays. If the teacher does not identify this misconception and provide the correct explanation, students can become very confused when trying to explain the seasons.

SOLO Taxonomy provides an opportunity to assess this prior knowledge and to address any misconceptions a student has. Two approaches can be taken:

1. breaking down global intentions under the SOLO levels for a unit of work (or topic), or

2. using the learning intentions from the learning log for individual lessons.

This section sets out examples of how each approach works.

Breaking down global intentions under SOLO levels

If your topic is seasons, you might break down the global intentions in the following way:

☐ **Uni/multistructural:** Identify the different seasons.

☐ **Relational:** Explain why these seasons occur at predictable times of the year.

☐ **Extended abstract:** Predict what would happen to the seasons if the earth's tilt was changed because of an impact from an asteroid.

You may then place these learning intentions into Template 2 on the next page and take the class through the following process:

1. Individually the students write what they know for each learning intention.

2. In small groups students share their answers. This is a good opportunity for them to have conversations and possibly to identify and correct misconceptions.

3. Hold a whole-class discussion, which may also highlight misconceptions. It is important to emphasise that it is okay for students to have limited knowledge about a topic especially if it is new to them.

4. Allow the students the opportunity to ask questions about the topic and to record these on the template.

With the students' questions, the teacher may:

☐ modify the learning intentions in teaching the unit or topic

☐ classify them under the SOLO levels and address them in the introductory lesson

☐ ask students to rank them according to the SOLO levels, and in this way encourage a sense that they have an input into what is being taught and that the process is a shared one.

Template 2: Measuring prior knowledge

Prior knowledge	
Unit/topic:	Name:

Global intentions:

Unistructural and multistructural:

Successfully identified one or several relevant facts ☐

Relational:

Successfully linked several facts together to explain their relationship ☐

Extended abstract:

Successfully linked the facts above to a new situation, context or concept ☐

Question(s) I would like answered about this topic:

Using learning intentions from the learning log

The second approach to assessing prior knowledge – using the learning intentions from the learning log – can be rewarding and fun. In a single lesson where a lesson intention has been broken down under the SOLO levels, the teacher can simply use questioning to draw out evidence of the students' prior knowledge. Alternatively any of the following strategies can be used for the same result:

1. **Think–pair–share:** Each student thinks of what they know about each level of the learning intention. They then share that information with a partner; in this activity it is also useful for the partner to repeat back to the speaker what they just said. Finally the pairs repeat the information they have shared to the whole class.

2. **Group share:** In groups of four, students work on a piece of paper divided into four quarters. Three of the quarters contain the three SOLO levels of the learning intention and the fourth is blank, where the students can write any questions they want answered. Each student has three minutes to write in a designated quarter. Again this information can then be shared with the whole class.

3. **Guess the word:** Each student is provided with a piece of paper containing a fact, idea, concept or process (which may be the same for multiple students) (Figure 7). The students keep their own piece of paper hidden so only they can see what is on it. They then have a minute to describe it to a partner; if their partner guesses what it is, the speaker gains a point. In the following minute the partners swap roles. The students then collect new cards and repeat this process three or four times. At the end of the activity, the student with the most points wins.

Figure 7: Sample "guess the word" cards to explore prior knowledge of seasons

Axis	Tilt
Summer	Winter
Season	Orbit
Hemisphere	Elliptical

6. Self assessment

Self assessment is a valuable tool for focusing students on their own abilities. A major factor influencing the value of this form of assessment is the accuracy with which a student can undertake it, and it is common sense to expect them to become more skilled at it with continued practice. As part of a wider assessment programme, self assessment can provide information and opportunities that the other methods cannot.

Self assessment is a great opportunity for students to evaluate their own performance. From this process the teacher can:

☐ gain insight into how the students view themselves

☐ identify any mismatch between the way the teacher and each student views the student's ability

☐ close any such gap in perceptions, which can have a powerful effect on student motivation and engagement

☐ more directly focus their conversations with a student in helping the student's perception to become more realistic.

The learning log provides the framework in which self assessment is seen as an integral and authentic part of students' learning in the classroom. It is important that students perceive self assessment in this way so that they can see the reason for investing cognitive effort in developing their skills in the process. As students become better at self assessment, they can use it to gain information on where they are, in relation to the learning log, and what they need to do in order to meet a defined success criterion in the learning log.

Figure 8 illustrates the relationship between the learning log and self assessment.

Figure 8: The learning log and self assessment

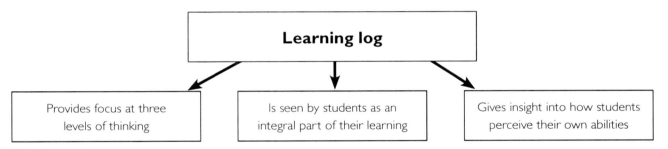

Methods of self assessment during a unit

The learning log can be used for self assessment in either of the following ways.

Method 1

1. The student identifies evidence in their book, or from another source, that they have achieved each of the learning intentions set out in the learning log.

2. The student codes the evidence, identifying it as U/M for uni/multistructural, R for relational and EA for extended abstract. They can also include colour-coding for easy identification.

3. The student compares their evidence against a rubric or exemplar which the teacher either has already prepared or models in the classroom.

4. The student ticks the appropriate success criteria for which they have provided evidence.

Method 2

1. The student identifies evidence for each of the learning intentions, coding them by SOLO level as in Method 1.

2. The student makes a value statement explaining how they assessed themselves against each success criterion.

For either of these methods, it is important that the teacher evaluates the accuracy of a student's self assessment and, if they identify discrepancies, discusses how these can be corrected. Class discussions based on any discrepancies noted are another valuable way of helping students learn how to self assess.

Generalised self assessment at the end of a unit

Another opportunity for self assessment is at the end of a unit or topic when students can undertake it in a more generalised way. In this process the student:

1. uses the global intentions, broken down into the SOLO levels (uni/multistructural, relational and extended abstract), to assess their own competence at each of the levels

2. ranks the SOLO verbs used in the unit, to establish their perceived competence with each of them

3. classifies facts, ideas, concepts or processes encountered in the unit in relation to their confidence with each of them

4. together with the teacher, creates goals based on this self assessment.

Example 11 below is a self assessment worksheet from a unit of work on electricity and magnetism. Thereafter Template 3 offers a generic format for any area of the curriculum.

Example 11: Self assessment worksheet for the end of a unit

Name:	Unit/topic: Electricity and magnetism

Global intentions *(1 = Very confident; 2 = Confident; 3 = Not confident)*
Uni/multistructural: Be able to define the terms electricity and magnetism. ☐
Relational: Be able to compare and contrast electricity and magnetism. ☐
Extended abstract: Be able to predict the effects of having no electricity on our lives. ☐

SOLO verbs
Rank the following verbs from 1 to 6 according to how difficult you find them to do.
(1 = Most difficult; 6 = Easiest)
Compare and contrast ☐   Define ☐   Describe ☐   Predict ☐   Relate ☐   Explain ☐

Facts, ideas, concepts or processes
Classify the terms listed below.

Understand	Some understanding	No understanding

Terms to be classified:

Electricity	Magnetism	Current	Amps	Negative	Static electricity	Closed circuit	Electromagnet
Conductor	Insulator	Lamp	Switch	Positive	Magnetic field	Parallel circuit	Series circuit
Volts	Watts	Poles	Mains	Electrons	Open circuit	Appliance	

Goals
Use the results of the self assessment activities above to create goals.
1.
2.
3.

Template 3: Generic format for self assessment at the end of a unit

Name:	Unit/topic:

Global intentions *(1 = Very confident; 2 = Confident; 3 = Not confident)*

Uni/multistructural:

Relational:

Extended abstract:

SOLO verbs

Rank the following verbs from 1 to 6 according to how difficult you find them to do.

(1 = Most difficult; 6 = Easiest)

Facts, ideas, concepts or processes

Classify the terms listed below.

Understand	Some understanding	No understanding

Terms to be classified:

Goals

Use the results of the self assessment activities above to create goals.

1.

2.

3.

7. Peer assessment

Peer assessment uses the interactions and conversations between students to identify misconceptions and areas of common difficulty. It provides the opportunity for students to help each other to close gaps in their understanding which a teacher may not have been able to do because of time constraints.

This collaborative process relies on students having learning-focused relationships. The learning log supports the process with a clear framework setting out what is expected from students. The SOLO verbs used throughout the log provide a common language on which to base learning conversations.

Peer assessment should not involve students awarding each other grades. Such an approach often leads to distractions in learning conversations, when students shift focus away from understanding where they are at and what they need to do to improve.

Students enjoy and value playing a part in assessment in the classroom. As with any new skill, they are likely to implement it poorly at first but to develop their skills with it over time. Figure 9 identifies the components that are needed to help establish effective peer assessment.

Figure 9: Components in effective peer assessment

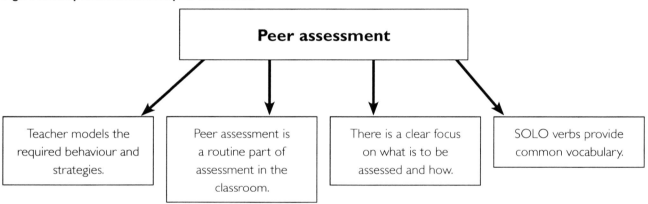

Another important feature of effective peer assessment is that students carry it out with a variety of students. By this means, they gain a broader range of views and perceptions of the work being assessed and further help in clarifying gaps in understanding.

Peer assessment based on the learning log can be approached in two ways:

1. individual learning intentions

2. extended answers.

Building individual learning intentions into peer assessment

As discussed in Section 6, individual learning intentions that have been broken down under the SOLO levels (uni/multistructural, relational and extended abstract) are used as part of the self assessment process. This process requires the student to identify and code evidence for each level of learning intention.

The next step is for students to peer assess against the learning intention at each SOLO level, which provides the opportunity to identify any differences in perception. During this process it is valuable for the teacher to:

☐ evaluate the accuracy of the peer assessment by asking for justification at each level of thinking

☐ ask the peer assessors to read out evidence they have provided for any of the levels to the whole class.

In Example 12 below, the learning intention at the extended abstract level has the potential to generate much discussion. Students could provide evidence for it in a number of ways including diagrams, modelling and role play.

Example 12: Learning intentions against which students peer assess

Learning intentions	
SLO 4: Know that shiny objects reflect light and that transparent objects refract light.	
Uni/multistructural	Recognise that shiny objects reflect light and transparent objects refract it.
Relational	Be able to explain why light can pass through some materials and not others.
Extended abstract	Predict what will happen to the speed of light in different media using an analogy.

Although initially students tend to feel uncomfortable with this collaborative approach to assessment, after a short period they no longer find it threatening and instead will ask for further opportunities to peer assess in this way.

Using extended answers in peer assessment

If students must provide an extended answer to a question such as "Is friction useful or not?", in which they have to provide evidence of their understanding at each level of thinking, they are forced to think carefully about the structure of their response. For a peer assessor it is potentially more difficult to identify the levels of thinking in this format because it has not been filtered or sequenced in the way they would expect to find in class notes.

The following two templates provide alternative ways of using extended answers in peer assessment:

☐ Template 4 provides no scaffolding for students and the peer assessor needs to first highlight evidence of each level of thinking and then make comments based on the quality of the evidence identified.

☐ Template 5 provides visual scaffolding with a box for each level of thinking. This method also makes it easier for the peer assessor who now only has to leave comments based on how they perceive the quality of evidence at each of the levels.

Template 4: Peer assessment worksheet (option A)

Question		
Evidence of uni/multistructural, relational and extended abstract	Extended answer	Comments

Template 5: Peer assessment worksheet (option B)

Question	
Uni/multistructural	Comments
Relational	Comments
Extended abstract	Comments

8. Tracking and progress

In my experience students' rate of progress can vary greatly which makes it difficult to measure it against a set standard. If a student has not reached the standard, they may lose motivation and consequently fall further behind. This experience can be very difficult to counteract especially if it has been reinforced on a number of occasions. At the other extreme, students who exceed a set standard can become complacent and lose motivation to make as much progress as they can. Moreover, a single student during their time at school could experience variable rates of progress due to influences such as their relationship with the teacher, level of interest in the topic or experiences of "aha" moments which lead to surges in progress.

A student's ability to focus on their own performance is very important. Students can waste a great deal of time and cognitive energy on comparing themselves with their peers. They can move away from such comparisons by drawing on the notion of **personal best**; here, as Andrew Martin describes it, students focus on achieving a benchmark (for a behaviour, skill or aspect of knowledge) that is better than or equal to their highest level of achievement in performance. Students can differ widely in their perception of excellence. By focusing on personal best, each student can see what excellence looks like for them and from there can set goals that are achievable in reaching their personal best.

I am aiming for my personal best. In the last unit I learnt how to define key concepts. In this unit I am aiming to relate those concepts to each other.

Tracking students' past and current performance provides information with which students can monitor their own progress. This information can also help a student in identifying when they have achieved a personal best.

Tracking can be used in a unit/topic (Templates 6 and 7) or throughout the entire year (Template 8). It can be done by using graphs (Template 7) or tables (Templates 6 and 8) or both.

The learning logs allow the teacher to track students according to the three SOLO levels of thinking (uni/multistructural, relational and extended abstract). They can provide information useful to teachers, students and parents. Using learning logs to track student progress offers the following advantages:

☐ Learning intentions that the student has not completed appear clearly in a graphic form, providing evidence that the teacher can pass on to the student and to parents and thus making the student more accountable.

☐ This method establishes a student's current performance and provides evidence of past performance, which supports the creation of goals for future performance.

☐ It provides the teacher with guidance on the teaching strategies they use.

☐ For students it can provide invaluable information on the success of a new learning behaviour or strategy.

☐ It provides the teacher with information they can use to vary the pace of instruction in ways that meet the student's current rate of progress.

Template 6: Tracking using a grid for a unit/topic

Unit/topic:			
Learning intention no.	Uni/multistructural	Relational	Extended abstract
1			
2			
3			
4			
5			
6			
7			
8			
9			
10			
11			
12			
13			

Template 7: Tracking using a graph for a unit/topic

Unit/topic: _____

	Uni/multistructural	Relational	Extended abstract
10			
9			
8			
7			
6			
5			
4			
3			
2			
1			

Learning intention number

Template 8: Year tracker

The student simply shades in the levels of thinking they successfully achieved.

Unit:									
Learning intention	1	2	3	4	5	6	7	8	9
Extended abstract									
Relational									
Uni/multistructural									
Unit:									
Learning intention	1	2	3	4	5	6	7	8	9
Extended abstract									
Relational									
Uni/multistructural									
Unit:									
Learning intention	1	2	3	4	5	6	7	8	9
Extended abstract									
Relational									
Uni/multistructural									
Unit:									
Learning intention	1	2	3	4	5	6	7	8	9
Extended abstract									
Relational									
Uni/multistructural									
Unit:									
Learning intention	1	2	3	4	5	6	7	8	9
Extended abstract									
Relational									
Uni/multistructural									

9.   The use of questions

An unexpected benefit of constructing questions using SOLO Taxonomy is that students rarely get an easy answer through using a search engine on the internet. While they can readily collect information related to a topic, idea or concept, they still have to use certain thinking skills to answer the question appropriately.

This principle can be taken a step further in a classroom context where students can access information from their exercise or textbooks, but still have to process information in order to answer or create a question.

The use of questions in the classroom can be viewed from two perspectives: the teacher's and the student's. Both of these viewpoints are outlined below.

Questions from the teacher

The learning log provides a focus for the type of questions that can be asked during a lesson or series of lessons. The teacher can base their questions on the different levels of learning intentions identified in the log, as indicated in Table 2.

Table 2: Questions to match the learning intentions at each SOLO level

SOLO level	Level of cognitive demand	Sample questions
Uni/multistructural	Relatively low	☐ What are the colours of the rainbow? ☐ Can you describe a concave mirror?
Relational	Somewhat higher, requiring students to connect ideas, facts or concepts	☐ How does the temperature of water relate to the percentage of dissolved oxygen? ☐ What are the similarities and differences between concave and convex mirrors?
Extended abstract	Most demanding	☐ Can you predict the effect of moving an object further away from a concave mirror? ☐ Can you form a hypothesis in relation to the effect of friction on objects with different types of surface?

Teachers tend to ask a lot of questions during a lesson. SOLO Taxonomy is a valuable tool they can use to analyse their approach to questioning. Knowing how many questions they have asked at each of the SOLO levels gives them important information on the level of challenge and guidance they are providing to students. For example, if a teacher is asking mainly uni/multistructural questions of a capable class, then they will be providing little challenge, and thus risking disengagement and a lack of interest in the topic.

Although differentiation in a classroom demands the use of all levels of thinking, the key is to establish the ratio of questions that suits the characteristics of each particular group of students. To gain the information you need to get the ratio right, create a record such as the one set out in Template 9 on the next page and ask two or three students to record all the questions you ask during a lesson. You can then use the results to reflect on the types of questions you asked.

Questions from students

The questions students ask can provide the teacher with important information. Analysis of these questions, using SOLO Taxonomy, can help in assessing a student's level of understanding. This is why it is essential to give students opportunities to formulate questions. Students should also be able to ask questions in a variety of ways, given that some prefer not to ask their questions publicly and some cannot think of questions quickly enough in a classroom environment.

Remember too that students themselves will gain important information from the process of formulating questions. The process provides them with another tool with which they can test their perceived level of understanding.

The examples on the following page illustrate three ways in which students can create their own questions based on the learning log and SOLO Taxonomy:

□ In Example 13, each student tries to create a question for each level of thinking within a single learning intention.

□ In Example 14, students again create their own question for each level of thinking but also include a question at each level from one of their peers. The peer's question can be identified through a class discussion or, if each student is to provide feedback on the other's question, a pairing exercise.

□ Creating questions with Example 15 involves a four-step process:

   – Each student creates three questions without identifying which level of SOLO they have created them for.

   – Each student collects a total of three questions, each one from a different person in the class, and records them in the table.

   – Each student categorises the questions they have collected under the different SOLO levels.

   – As a whole class or in pairs, students justify and defend their classification of the questions (keeping the authors of the questions anonymous).

Template 9: Log of teacher's questions

Learning intention:	Date:
Student (*In the space provided below, record all the questions the teacher asks during the lesson.*)	Teacher (*Categorise each question as uni/multistructural, relational or extended abstract.*)
Teacher's reflection	

Example 13: Student questions at three levels of thinking

Learning intentions	
SLO 6: Understand what friction is and how it can be observed in everyday life.	
Uni/multistructural	Be able to define the term *friction*.
Question	
Relational	Be able to explain how friction affects us in our everyday lives and how its effects can be reduced.
Question	
Extended abstract	Be able to predict how mass, type of surface and contact area affect the amount of friction.
Question	

Example 14: Student and peer questions at three levels of thinking

Learning intentions	
SLO 6: Understand what friction is and how it can be observed in everyday life.	
Uni/multistructural	Be able to define the term *friction*.
My question	
Peer's question	
Relational	Be able to explain how friction affects us in our everyday lives and how its effects can be reduced.
My question	
Peer's question	
Extended abstract	Be able to predict how mass, type of surface and contact area affect the amount of friction.
My question	
Peer's question	

Example 15: Matching student questions to the appropriate level of thinking

Question	My categorisation
1.	Uni/multistructural Relational Extended abstract
2.	Uni/multistructural Relational Extended abstract
3.	Uni/multistructural Relational Extended abstract
Justification	
Question 1:	
Question 2:	
Question 3:	

10. Lesson planning

Teaching is a responsive and fluid activity in which the teacher has to be adaptable and creative in order to meet the learning demands of the students. It always involves an element of unpredictability because so many factors can influence students' responsiveness and engagement. A lesson plan therefore is not meant to be a script that is implemented exactly as it is written because such a script would not take into account the variety in the pace of students' learning. Instead an effective lesson plan provides a framework that helps a teacher deal with this variability.

Elements of a lesson plan

The learning intentions identified in the learning log provide a clear starting point for planning lessons. The SOLO levels provide scaffolding on which to develop opportunities to achieve the learning intention at each level. This differentiated approach allows students to be challenged appropriately and identifies the formative assessment opportunities that will support them at each level of the learning intentions.

By assessing prior knowledge, the teacher can gain important information that can influence their choice of instructional techniques and the pace of the lesson. The lesson plan needs to provide flexibility in how the teacher reacts to these demands while maintaining a clear focus on the learning intentions.

Students often perceive lessons as disconnected from each other and fail to see the links and progression in the content over a series of lessons. It is important that the teacher makes these links obvious and introduces a routine that encourages students to reflect on the relationships among the lessons.

ICT can be a powerful tool in the learning process and greater engagement often results from its use. However, if its role in the learning process is unclear it can fail to engage students. Identifying the ICT interventions and what level of the learning intentions they support provides legitimacy to their use.

A lesson plan written in relation to SOLO Taxonomy provides a clear and structured framework for the teacher to reflect on. Figure 10 presents some questions that the teacher could use in that reflective process.

Figure 10: Questions for teacher reflection

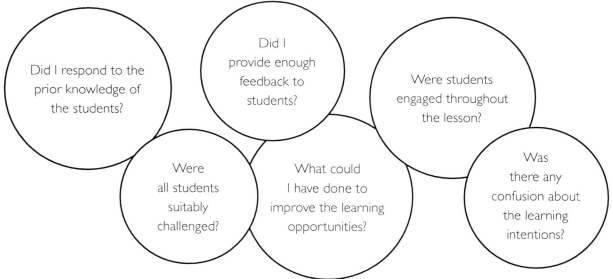

This reflective process can then be used to set goals, helping to maintain a focus on those areas that need improvement.

Example 16 shows a flexible lesson plan that has been built around the framework of SOLO Taxonomy. Thereafter Template 10 offers a generic format for planning in any area of the curriculum.

Example 16: SOLO lesson plan for earth science class

Topic: Earth in space	Room: G21		Class: 10Z
Learning intentions		Success criteria	
Uni/multistructural Be able to define the term *seasons*. Relational Know the seasons are caused by the earth's revolution and its tilt. Extended abstract Be able to predict how seasons will vary between countries based on their position relative to the equator.		Uni/multistructural I can define the term *seasons*. Relational I can explain how the earth's revolution and tilt cause the seasons. Extended abstract I can predict how seasons will vary between countries relative to their position to the equator.	

Previous lesson: Earth's rotation; orbit of earth around the sun

Prior knowledge: "Guess the word" activity (see Section 5)

Modelling (scientific content)		Modelling (SOLO verbs)
Revolution	Earth's tilt	Process of making a prediction

Learning opportunities		
Uni/multistructural	Relational	Extended abstract
Cloze activity with key terms and ideas		
Demonstration and modelling: Earth's rotation and orbit around the sun and relate to seasons		
Practical activity: Measuring angle of light source and recording its effect on temperature		
Modelling: Process to develop a prediction Predict: If seasons vary between countries		

ICT opportunities		
Uni/multistructural	Relational	Extended abstract
www.wallwisher.com for students to share definitions		
Videos from www.youtube.com that demonstrate the earth's rotation and orbit round the sun		
Using www.voicethread students share how they justify their predictions		

Next lesson: Earth–sun–moon model; the relationship between the moon and earth

Reflection
The teacher reflects on various aspects of the class including: ☐ success criteria   ☐ levels of response from students in relation to SOLO ☐ engagement   ☐ management. ☐ timing **Goals:** Use the outcome of this reflection to develop goals. 1. 2. 3

Template 10: SOLO lesson plan

Topic:	Room:	Class:

Learning intentions		Success criteria	
Uni/multistructural Relational Extended abstract		Uni/multistructural Relational Extended abstract	

Previous lesson

Prior knowledge

Modelling (content)		Modelling (SOLO verbs)	

Learning opportunities		
Uni/multistructural	Relational	Extended abstract

ICT opportunities		
Uni/multistructural	Relational	Extended abstract

Next lesson

Reflection

Goals

1.

2.

3

11. The impact of SOLO Taxonomy and the learning log

The ultimate wish of all involved in education is to maximise the potential of and improve outcomes for all students. In this final section I will present information that indicates how SOLO and the learning log impact on teachers and students. After presenting some quantitative data, I present the perceptions of some teachers and students.

The perceptions and data were collected from teachers and students from two secondary schools in New Zealand. The students range in age from 14 to 18 years. In New Zealand's standards-based assessment system, students complete multiple units of work across various curricula, each leading to a grade of Not Achieved, Achieved, Merit or Excellence.

Quantitative data

The following data were collected from samples of students ranging from in number 30 to 60. They compare pre and post SOLO results for the same end of topic test, with the pre-SOLO data averaged over three years. They show that there is potential for all students, whatever their ability, to benefit from the use of SOLO Taxonomy and the learning logs.

In a **Year 9** class:

- the proportion of students graded Achieved rose from 26% to 41% after the introduction of the SOLO method
- the proportion of students graded at the higher levels of Merit and Excellence increased between 3% and 6%.

These results were mirrored in another class, in which the proportion of students reaching Achieved increased from 3% to 32% through successive end of topic tests.

In **Year 10**:

- the proportion of students attaining a grade of Achieved fell from 22% to 6%
- the proportion of students attaining a grade of Merit fell from 74% to 64%
- critically the proportion of students attaining a grade of Excellence rose dramatically from 3% to 30%.

In **Year 12**:

- the proportion of students who were attaining intermediate grades of Achieved and Merit fell from 35% to 19%
- the proportion of students at the highest level of Excellence increased significantly from 9% to 39%.

Perceptions from teachers

Teachers' reflections on their use of SOLO Taxonomy include the following:

- "Students now have a clearer understanding of what is expected in terms of depth of thinking and what it looks like to be successful."
- "I am engaging my students more effectively and have raised their expectations in what they can achieve."
- "We now have a clear understanding of how to differentiate for our students that provides a personalised learning path."
- "We have found low achievers are encouraged to stretch their learning when they enjoy success achieving success criteria."
- "The learning logs made it easier for learners to evaluate and make judgements about the quality of their work."
- "The teacher and learner have a framework to monitor progress."

Perceptions from students

Review of Teaching through the Solo Taxonomy of Thinking

For the past two years, I have become accustomed to an entirely new way of thinking through the SOLO Taxonomy of thinking introduced to us in science. Initially I had a strong aversion towards it. However, having noticed the immense pedagogical implications behind this scheme, I am now fairly open to such learning.

The SOLO Taxonomy of thinking incorporates three levels of thinking that form the basis of the learning intention [for] each lesson. The first is multistructural. Most teaching merely extends to this level as teachers drone on about facts that attain little significance in the bigger picture. This is followed by the "relational" level in which logical links between facts are established giving them greater relevance and educational value. Finally the extended abstract level challenges us to think more in depth about the relationship between things whether it be every day implications, generalisations evaluation and prediction. Together this outline stimulates in depth thought and analytical skills that ultimately generates higher level cognitive function.

My initial response to the introduction of the Solo Taxonomy was far from enthusiastic. Though I was entirely capable, teachers rarely demand students to use their brain to such capacity. I only accepted it once I found it accountable for my near perfect results in all the subjects in the end of year exam.

The fact that each lesson is broken down into these levels directly relating to what we are learning enables us to learn far more than what is outlined in the syllabus. Far greater interest is generated in learning as we are taught to recognise the significance in the seemingly meaningless information. The downfall of this, is of course the time it takes to do these things but again this forces us to work faster and achieve more in the space that ordinary classes may have merely covered the basics in.

The use of other devices generates further interest where conventional teaching fails to capture our attention. It is often very difficult to focus on in depth thinking when it is far easier to remain ignorant. Thus, Mr Martin keeps our interest by offering us variation such as the opportunity to carry out practical experiments and do individual research on the internet. For many students who struggle to stay focused, this is a brilliant means of capturing our interest.

Furthermore, the structure of the lesson itself in which Mr Martin facilitates us with the learning intention – and the internet if we're lucky – allows us to do the work and then interrogates us about our answers afterwards, is personally quite frustrating, but it too attains significant educational benefit. To every student's dismay, but to their educational benefit nonetheless, the lesson structure restricts socialising to frantic searching for answers between one another; answers that we know Mr Martin will persistently demand at the end of the lesson. For most of us, this pressure is the greatest demand for deeper level thinking.

Overall, the SOLO Taxonomy of thinking is one of the most influential skills I have acquired in my education as of yet and I have found it the greatest distinction between achievement in primary and secondary school. Despite the initial frustration I now utilise the skills in almost all subjects at school and beyond. Consequently, I believe it to be accountable for a significant improvement and consistency in my grades. Should this be applied to the education of other students, I believe there is no doubt that it will yield similar results.

Lesson Feedback

Previously, my science classroom would run like any other; it was a practical classroom that met the New Zealand Curriculum and would teach students the necessities of achieving in the topic. There would be both practical and theory tasks and provided resources so students could carry out investigations. However, the lessons would only meet the requirements of the topic, not often extending students and applying what they have learnt to real situations. When I started in my new classroom, a variety of new learning techniques including SOLO Taxonomy, virtual lessons and SLO learning objectives had been introduced.

Whenever students are assigned to explain a scientific concept, they are often using SOLO Taxonomy. It is the Structure of Observed Learning Outcomes and consists of four main stages in which information is distributed. It helps develop what students have learnt and to apply it in a variety of levels. The unistructural and multistructural stages help identify several statements that are relevant to the topic. The relational stage takes these statements and ideas and links them to a whole. It often sequences, classifies, compares and contrasts the topic. The extended abstract stage aims to give an overall generalisation of the given topic. It gives an evaluation and personal opinion and can link ideas to the future, whilst making measurable predictions and identifying how the idea is impacting on our world. This particular stage enables students to go beyond and to extend themselves in their learning. In more advanced classes, students will be aiming to achieve at this stage, whilst in other classes the relational stage would be targeted the most.

On a variety of occasions, students have access to a variety of resources which enable them to participate in virtual lessons. These are lessons that have been planned out by teachers that allow students to contribute in a planned lesson either online or on a computer. Netbooks and laptops are used amongst students so that they participate in quizzes, lessons, further research and animations, including GoAnimate. GoAnimate is a website that allows students to express information relating to a scientific subject. Analogies are often used as examples to convey information. This not only shows a student's scientific understanding, but [allows them] to also apply information so that others can understand and are well informed.

At the beginning of each class, every student receives an SLO sheet which contains the day's learning objectives and success criteria. This is linked to the SOLO Taxonomy which helps students understand the intentions of the day's lesson as well as informing them about what they should be able to achieve. Each SLO has several boxes which are ticked once the objective has been learnt. Evidence in students' books is often noted. This is a good way the teacher can see who has achieved the objectives and who needs help. Each SLO is carefully followed out, either with a practical or theory and followed with a conclusion and discussion.

Overall, the new learning techniques have benefited me and the class tremendously. The impact of SOLO Taxonomy and the virtual lessons encourages students to extend themselves and to be open-minded in their learning. The variety of resources enables students to express their creativity as well as their scientific knowledge. The use of analogies in discussions gets students involved and motivated towards their own learning. The lessons are both informative and enjoyable whilst [setting] challenges [to] pupils to think outside the box. This type of learning has certainly benefited our learning environment. Hopefully in future many more classes can contribute in this new learning experience.

Conclusion

This book set out to demonstrate how SOLO Taxonomy can be used as a framework for teaching and learning. The learning intentions and success criteria established under the levels of SOLO in the learning log provide the challenge and clarity needed for students to experience success. The process of creating learning intentions and success criteria using SOLO gets easier with practice, and with it the teacher has a focus for developing their own thinking on SOLO cognitive processing. The framework established by SOLO Taxonomy and the learning log provides:

- ☐ access to effective differentiation
- ☐ a means of self and peer assessment
- ☐ a method of measuring prior knowledge
- ☐ a way to provide effective feedback and feed forward
- ☐ a means of measuring and identifying progress
- ☐ importantly a framework that a teacher can use to measure their own impact on students' learning.

I hope that the resources offered in this book will help you and your students along a richly rewarding SOLO journey of your own.

Lightning Source UK Ltd.
Milton Keynes UK
UKOW012023131212

203631UK00003B/21/P